Woman Drinking Absinthe

Woman Drinking Absinthe

Katherine E. Young

Alan Squire Publishing
Bethesda, Maryland

Alan Squire Publishing

Woman Drinking Absinthe is published by Alan Squire Publishing, Bethesda, MD, an imprint of the Santa Fe Writers Project.

Printed in the United States of America.
ISBN (print): 978-1-942892-24-3
ISBN (epub): 978-1-942892-25-0
Library of Congress Control Number: 2020945411

Cover painting by Henri de Toulouse-Lautrec, *Waiting*. Image courtesy Clark Art Institute, clarkart.edu.

Jacket design by Randy Stanard, Dewitt Designs, www.dewittdesigns.com.

Author photo by Samantha H. Collins.

Copy editing and interior design by Nita Congress.

Printing consultant: Steven Waxman.

Printed by API Print Productions.

First Edition
Ordo Vagorum

Acknowledgments

Grateful acknowledgment is made to the editors of these publications, in which the following poems appeared in earlier form:

Anomaly: "Planning Your Suburban Affair"

Connotation Press: An Online Artifact: "Leaving Home" and "Postcards from the Floating World"

Gargoyle: "Bluebeard," "Calculus," "Succuba," and "Today I'm Writing Love Songs"

Poets Are Present Anthology (Washington Shakespeare Theatre): "Bar at the Folies-Bergère"

Prairie Schooner: "African Violets" and "The Bear"

Prime Number: "Soul Food"

Rosebud: "Interval"

Sou'wester: "Euclidean Geometry"

Subtropics: "Dénouement"

Tampa Review: "If There Is a Hell"

TAB: The Journal of Poetry & Poetics: "Plane Angle"

Taos Journal of International Poetry and Art: "Nakhla" and "A Receipt to Cure Mad Dogs, or Men or Beasts Bitten by Mad Dogs"

Valparaiso Poetry Review: "Birdsong"

"Bar at the Folies-Bergère" was commissioned by the Washington Shakespeare Theatre as part of its Poets Are Present residency.

"Bar at the Folies-Bergère" and "Dénouement" also appeared in *Arlington Literary Journal*.

"Interval" also appeared in the Sterling A. Brown Tribute Issue of *Beltway Poetry Quarterly*.

I am profoundly grateful to Hailey Leithauser and Richard Peabody for support, encouragement, and (sometimes) commiseration as this manuscript journeyed through the world. Thanks to Rabab Ahmed and Sushmita Mazumdar for their help with Bengali and to Michael A. Schaffner for sharing his expertise on the American Civil War. Thanks also to my friends and colleagues at the University of Maryland, College Park, where many of these poems were conceived. Special thanks to Jocelyn Heath for the gift of her poetry, and especially for her friendship. Thanks to Barbara Roesmann, friend.

Contents

IV.

V.

I.

Birdsong

Silken hour: a cat rattles the blinds,
thumps across your chest,
bats at your eyelids.
Weaving through what might be
a dream, the thread of a story,
you hear the voice of someone
who once seemed unimportant
whispering now "How fine you are!"
The words vibrate along your inner string,
resonate strong and clear before
dissolving to birdsong:
shriek and whistle,
careless click-clack of beaks,
the shaping of the empty air.
You say to your husband
quite matter-of-factly,
"I dreamed of X,"
and he laughs, day begins.

The Bear

i.

The bear marauds inside my garden,
plants his tracks among the roses;
his scent lingers in the hollies, the yews.
I gather broken branches in my arms,
pocking hands and face with prickling leaves.
Inside the house, my cats sniff anxiously,
note the bitter tang of bear on my skin.
They press their noses to the window,
seeking solace in the glass:
clear-eyed frame that holds us back,
bladed pane that keeps us safe.

4

ii.

The bear says: "I'm not dangerous!
Let me make a den for you:
I'll decorate the walls with shells,
spread soft moss across your bed;
songs of falling water will soothe the air.
Sometimes—perhaps—I'll kiss
your full, pleading lips,
though they're not the type
to which I'm accustomed."

iii.

I tell the bear: "My prince
will come claim me." Clear, uninflected.
The bear just laughs:
"Does his skin smell of musk,
his flesh taste of honey?
Does his fur warm you in winter?
Does he know to smooth your cheek
with all his claws drawn in?"

iv.

When he holds me in his arms,
I hear roaring in my ear.

V.

The bear says, "Look closely:
there's a ring set in my nose."
And though I've stroked his snout
a thousand times, I've never—before now—
felt iron beneath my fingers.
Says the bear, "Once, I begged
for my living, recited rhymes,
my paw outstretched.
I screwed the ring in myself,
thought I'd live better with a chain,
with four walls to steady me."

vi.

The bear shambles through crowds,
snout turning side to side,
his eyes always seeking,
I don't know what he's seeking…
He prefers I fall two steps back,
that way no one shouts, "Look!
A woman's chained to that bear!"
Although the chain's invisible.
Although at night, when he leads me out,
no one sees he's a bear.

Interval

You say that "interval"
means the space between
our two notes, structure
of a chord in a tune
by Monk: you think in jazz.
Your heartbeats riff, solo, jam.
You seek syncopation,
seek collaboration,
seek concatenation.
"Emotion" and "flow"
are your middle names.

Your last life, you sat in once
with Mingus, felt him
lay down that groove,
your hands, lips, whole body
poised to pass it on.
"I'm a sensual man,"
you say to me as you stroke
my keys, pluck
my catgut strings, blow
Coltrane through my bones.

Nakhla

Perhaps it begins in Egypt, heralded
by thunderbolts: things

that fall from the sky always have meaning.
Tang of scorched flesh, fur.

Fear. A farmer points to the spot
where his dog was just standing,

howling perhaps at Unkind Fate,
which leaves no trace of him—

not even a bone to bury him by.
Perhaps it begins millions

of years ago, time of soft-bodied
creatures, jellyfish, worms,

time when a planet's passions cool,
harden to stone. Time

when shells accrete, when trilobites
scissor free from pouches,

when a cousin of the nautilus
first fuses tentacles

to spadix, passes sperm to the female
during lazy, day-long

couplings in a gentle sea.
Perhaps it begins on Mars

as magma cools itself to crystal,
when water splits that crystal,

veins the cracks with carbonate.
Perhaps it begins when

an unknown force slams into Mars,
blasting that rock out

into space.
            Ten million years go by:
oceans fall, mountains

rise, and Lucy *Australopithecus*
chooses her mate. Now

we come to Egypt; a farmer whistles
for his dog. At this moment,

a twenty-two-pound Martian rock
shrieks overhead, shatters

in fire above the Nile. Proof—
if any's needed—that what's

essential to both blood and bone
travels the planets: calcium,

iron, magnesium, silver
elements that stiffen

shell and skeleton, that bind
and carry oxygen,

that transmit sense from nerve to straining
nerve—pulse and gasp,

ebb and flow, rhythm of
two human hearts.
                              Perhaps

it begins this instant as I lay
my body over yours,

bone rocking bone, tooth skimming skin,
night sky of summer exploding

above us. Silver-white, malleable:
stars figure your face.

Salt

Not like sun sinking
in vermilion cloud,

nor moon sailing
a silver-brushed sea,

not like waves shushing
mutinous seabirds,

nor dew beading
a web, not agelessly,

not immortally
—though I, too, am these—

but simply, as in the story
of the woman who

counts her devotion
in grains of salt,

seasoning
that gives life its savor:

that's what I'll be
for you, o love.

14

Euclidean Geometry

A *point* is that which has no part.
       Coordinates: how we constellate a sky.

A *line* is breadthless length.
       Our line's intangible, then—it's still a line.

The ends of a line are points.
       You and I form a unity of two.

A *straight line* is a line that lies evenly with the points on itself.
       Our line won't deviate; our line lies true.

A *surface* is that which has length and breadth only.
       We map our perimeter—each finger leaves its print.

The edges of a surface are lines.
       Curve of my cheek. Slant of your eye.

A *boundary* is that which is an extremity of anything.
       What we construct. How each holds the other in.

A *figure* is that which is contained by any boundary or boundaries.
       Interplay of planes: our smooth-surfaced skin.

A *circle* is a plane figure contained by one line.
       Flaw defying logic: both beginning and end.

II.

Today I'm Writing Love Songs

after Marina Tsvetayeva

Today I'm writing love songs, Marina,
as if you yourself had written none, as if
no other woman ever felt or smelled
or tasted love's ripe flesh, never stripped
love's husk to find succor within until I,
arriving with my hand outstretched,
plucked at it from idle curiosity.

I promise, Marina, I'll savor this love whole,
run my lips along its rim, swallow
juices, rind, pips, drink in each drop as if
it's the last. Passion slips from its skin, dissolves
sweet, hot, sour, bitter, salty on my tongue,
recalling foods fashioned by the ancients,
who stirred seeds of love in their cooking pots.

They say I look young again, Marina,
my skin's furrows softened by gentle rain.
But you and I, we descend from monsoon—
our sort of love engorges the river,
corduroys the fields, drowns the seedlings
asleep in cradling earth. Heat, water, ooze,
fruit rotting in mud: no haven's safe from us.

Planning Your Suburban Affair

You'll need a map, though there's no substitute
for local knowledge. Consider the parks, scout
their parking lots: note any trees that screen.
Walk the quieter paths, hear mulch crackle,
cock an ear for barking dogs. Check shrubs
for cover, picnic shelters—you never know
when it might rain. Weigh the likelihood
of snakes against the certainty of joggers.
Buy condoms at a place where they don't keep
your prescriptions on file, where you won't meet
the checkout clerk at back-to-school night.
Quick, think what you'll say when someone rifles
your purse for stamps: "Let me, hon, you never
find anything in there!" Take up yoga,
poetry, something to get you out at night.
Now you're off, eyes conning the dark. You seek
the hole between lampposts: bone in the throat
of the universe that buys you time. Watch how
cars flow, see their headlights sweep the shadows.
Check your pulse, register its spasm;
take off your wedding ring. Pack a flashlight, fine,
but you can't ever turn it on.

Plane Angle

after Euclid

We have the angle: you, me. We can't yet
determine its inclination: acute? Obtuse?

There are other angles—husbands, wives,
the woman up in Boston you see twice

a year on business—our configuration's
multidimensional. From our single

point of intersection, lines radiate out:
children, parents, siblings, neighbors, friends.

In bookstores, bars, restaurants, and malls,
we masquerade as ordinary folk

whose shoes need polishing. We know no one's
ever embodied divinity the way

we do, initiates stealing to darkened
parking lots as if to the bridal bed.

Trailing behind, our individual lines
contort, constructing triangles, cones, circles,

starbursts that strike sparks from concrete berms,
tiled walks in raucous shivaree—as if

tomorrow at dawn our loved ones will break down
the door, parade the bloodstained sheets through town.

Home Visit

"I want you to meet my family,"
he'd said to his new lover.

Now she stood in his living room:
the man she loved smiling,

inexplicably at ease,
the younger son staring,

the older not lifting his eyes
from his computer screen,

and, chatting randomly about backsplash
and tile while she steeped tea,

the wife, who'd clearly taken pains
to tidy up the place.

Succuba

Imprisoned in the kitchen herbs—
rosemary, lavender, wormwood—

by day I haunt your close-clipped lawn,
the fruiting trees that edge your land.

Sometimes I tiptoe to your window,
watch your children play within.

Evenings you walk out in the yard,
woman dangling from your arm.

Late at night you come alone,
pressing berries in my fingers,

smearing honey on my breasts:
mouthing greedily, you curse me.

Take up your snakeskin now, my love,
twine it among the needled greens,

the nest of wasps, the holly leaves,
objects you hang to guard your door—

when the appointed moment comes,
all charms will fail, fall useless from

your hands: this witch already dwells
within, blue lips telling the hours.

Calculus

And they're picking at sushi and talking like people who
  don't know
each other well but mean to and aren't so sure of the rules
  anymore

because the old rules covered things like a girl not talking
  dirty
and backseat kissing and all the places she shouldn't let
  him put his hands

but this new talk needs new rules, now he's quoting his
  therapist
and she's saying he should leave his wife *now*, she's
  saying staying's worse

and both of them are draining glasses, mounding napkins,
  flicking chopsticks
so as not to accidentally glimpse the slits that can ghost
  across wrists

because here, in this talk, the husbands are shouting,
  they're slapping
not-so-secret lovers, while at home the wives are
  screaming

and the children have been stayed together for, and their
    savage, selfish eyes
let no one forget it, while their fathers are screaming

as their mothers take lovers whom they're kissing in cars,
    hands bruising
in motion as breath stutters, sobs, approaches infinity

If There Is a Hell

it resembles this street in shadow, this street
and this streetlamp, where you and I cling

so tightly our flesh bruises for weeks and
our mouths ache with the work of longing

it blinks cold, disapproving, like stars glimpsed
from hard ground as muscle grinds into grit

it feels, like your fingers, for tears on my cheek

it tastes of tea brewed by your wife, shakes
like her hand as she pours a cup for me

it kisses like my husband scenting you
on my lips, hunches his shoulders as if he might care

it cries like my son at my step on the stair,
as he finds he's stayed awake, after all

Dénouement

In this final scene, my son's on stage,
bouncing his ball beneath the hoop,
berating himself with every miss.
A spotlight circumscribes his world:
foul line scuffed between the beds,
basket adjusted to just his height,
chicken wire strung up to save
the neighbors' roses. Here in the wings,
a lover beats me black and blue.
Soon he'll shove me back before
the footlights, where the actor playing
my husband will rouse himself, bemused,
finger my bruises, disconnect
on cue. I'll exit, towel off
my pancake base, peel back my lashes
in the green room mirror. Meanwhile,
the Awful Messenger arrives,
speaks his lines to my son, who's
already screaming as shot after
errant shot ricochets into
the plastic phlox, the black-eyed susans.

III.

Leaving Home

Leaving home—my husband's house—
I lose myself, baffled by streets
bearing names I no longer know,
their curves and contours couched in shadow,
each Eden, El Dorado, Elysium
a sign signaling simply "Exit."
Slipping beneath the city's skin,
I discover bluegrass, blues, jazz bars,
burr of Scotch, whisky with soda,
I meet a man—many men—
feel fingers flense my face, smell
the way flesh melts into midnight
in temporary rooms. Recently,
I dreamed of home, my husband's back
partitioning the bed: unbreached,
unbreachable. Here, when it rains,
the skylight weeps; the sink gnaws
its own enamel. Near the window,
an amaryllis arrays itself
anxiously. "So much need,"
my husband once said, in disbelief—
so much needless grief.

The Golden Fish

Some say I'm a fish, some a mermaid;
the women say I'm something worse.
What's important: I enthrall
the fishermen, arrest their knives
at the point of entry. Chinese, English,
Russian, all the common tongues:
it isn't hard to learn the words
to ask these men, "What's your desire?"
Each thinks I speak to him alone.
Each says the same thing: peace at home,
the wife's forgotten how much
he loves her, what she wants is stuff
(funny—these men just want to fish).
Once I give him what he wants,
the clever wife gets what she wants:
granite counters, induction burners—
she's lady, tsarina, queen of hearts.
(Does she ever deign to thank me?
Ever imagine *her* life with fins?)
After a while, a squall blows up—
he's sorry, the man tells me, his wife's
gone crazy, she wants to be—God.
Could I, please, just one last time—?
Some things don't even require
enchantment. "Go home now," I sigh
(I always sigh): "she's waiting by
the door once more." He's gone, just
like that: they never come back.

African Violets

February ushers in winter's rain,
teasing the boxwoods, the trellis roses
nodding in the yard. A lonely crocus
raises its head, unable to refrain
despite lingering snow, silvery scrim
mantling the sun. Houseplants sink into
melancholy, recline swooning on window
frames cracked and swollen from the heat within.
Early mornings I tend them, sprinkle cool
water on their petals; their parched, pale leaves
nuzzle against my hand. Like young children,
like new lovers, they've no better sense
than to seek my caress: they must believe
in old wives' tales, promise of renewal.

Bar at the Folies-Bergère

It starts with the scent of lavender as she
buttons clean pantaloons, laces up stays,
smooths her bodice and shakes out the frills,
ties the black ribbon about her neck.
Her costume smells, as they all do: mingled
sweat and makeup, the fabric itself,
splashed, perhaps, with the licorice twist of absinthe.
Then come powder and rouge, the small earrings,
a pink and white corsage already starting
to droop. Her props are placed on view: beer bottles,
champagne, a vase containing two pale roses,
cut-glass bowl of oranges that may
or may not indicate a certain kind
of availability. Leaning against
the marble bar, she doesn't look at you
(Why should she look at you? Can you give her
what she needs, or even cab fare home?):
posing, perhaps, or perhaps beyond posing,
her face bleak, artificially rosy amid
the moon-pale globes and crystals shimmering
in the ersatz heaven of the cabaret.
Perhaps a man inspects her in the glass,
perhaps he's looking past; neither of them
seems to see the woman on the trapeze,
feet squeezed into ankle boots of lizard green.
Later, she observes his red-gold lashes,

watches his still-young face slacken in sleep,
breathes in his scent of cigars, cheap brandy,
scent that clings to her fingers like orange oil
as she works her nails beneath the skin,
methodically stripping the pith to find
whatever's left of the fruit's sweet flesh.

Woman Drinking Absinthe

"A living man is blind and drinks his drop."
— WB Yeats

Tonight you're speaking of your wife,
the bride you brought across the sea:
she tends your sons, pickles fish
and ginger on weekends, teaches
you the custom of her father,
who kept a woman in the village.

The waitress knows us as a pair:
we share a glass, finish one
another's sentences. But what's
my role in this miserable tableau—
girlfriend? whore?—pursing my lips
in the brass cladding of the bar…

I've pitched into your blind man's ditch—
Toulouse-Lautrec might've cartooned
the blowzy hair, the cloudy gaze
of the woman at this table coaxing
one last drop from *la fée verte*,
one last delusion from the muse.

You shrug, obligingly peel back flaps:
cloth, skin, connective tissue, rib.
So framed, your heart glistens like
the frog's: ghastly hallucination.
I gaze at its pulsing, nacreous sac—
so like my own?—tell myself

"This must be love." Already I've
succumbed to viridescent dreams—
numbed myself to fingers fumbling
at bra straps, clasps, the cup and suction
of your mouth, the weals it leaves—*louche*
of bitter wormwood, of aniseed.

Bluebeard

His beard was blue, but not so very blue.
So when he handed me his keys

and warned me not to try the littlest one,
I fingered the scrolls that curled along

its bow, its tiny nape and teeth, and hung it
from a silk ribbon above my heart.

I tidied the rooms while he was gone, oiling
the other locks, their keys. So what

if I tripped over objects in the gloom,
sent them spinning toward dim corners?

Of course they weren't bones! As for the iron-
sweet scent of blood in the air—it must

have been my own. Besides, a woman needn't
fear blood or bones, touchstones she's learned

to reckon by—how else could she simmer
stock from her body's blossom, coax

fresh, new growth from the very marrow of life?
At last he returned, roaring through

the door, tearing cloth and wire to free
the key dangling between my breasts,

sniff it suspiciously. Oddly arousing:
his pouting, disappointed mouth.

Postcards from the Floating World

I cry out. His words
fall, petals on the ocean,
blossoms in a storm.

ii.

I cry out. His eyes
flicker, luckless, entangled
in the streetlight's net.

iii.

I cry out. His lips
fold up like birds' broken wings
tensed against his mouth.

iv.

I cry out. His hands
claw fierce, wild, deeper than pain
cradling my face.

Soul Food

That first time when you hit me,
I marveled at the *crack*

your hand made as it struck
flat against my face.

I should have known right then:
we were headed straight

for this soul food joint where
I'm picking at turnip greens,

sweet potato pie,
as you plead with me to take

my inconvenient heart
and just go away.

You say it's all my fault:
I ask too much, love

too deep. "Don't make me do it
again," you say. I know

you mean it. Like you mean
this next thing: when we've split

44

the last of the cornbread, made
our exit past the catfish

gazing lugubrious
in his tank, when we're standing

in the parking lot, your arms
around me, your hand—same hand—

traces the bone of my cheek,
softly, longingly,

as if I'd never been there,
as if you'd never leave.

45

IV.

Place of Peace

Shiloh National Military Park
for Alexander

i.

Mississippi's an enigma: the road
unrolling car-free, wooden crosses cluttering

close-clipped lawns. Those small, mournful towns
with odd, exquisite names: Senatobia,

Toccopola, Geeville. Courthouse squares
where the lone Confederate soldier

achieves apotheosis. I order coffee
in Corinth without meeting a living soul

besides the woman at the counter who startles
from her magazine when I rattle the screen.

At the local Civil War museum, maps
show how the rail line south to New Orleans

bisects the main track east, right here, in Corinth:
the battle's object, the whole point of the thing.

ii.

The point of any pilgrimage: to ask
why. Crossing into Tennessee, I find

all the cars missing along the highway
congregated in the parking lot;

I stand in line for tickets, for bottled water.
Near the reconstructed Meeting House,

boys punch one another: sharp, feral
jabs after hours in a minivan.

Like other pilgrims before us here, we mark
our passage on this land, rutting the hills

with the wheels of our SUVs, commingling
ancient with modern, pretzel wrappers, earbuds,

bug spray with the eternal question, why,
as if answers might lie in the trees, the stones.

iii.

Trees and stones: campsites, split rail fences,
country lanes. Age-old armies spring up,

arrayed along the ridges, clustered among
the fields. Ghosts abandon their bivouacs

to jostle among us, here and not here,
past blending into present, it's almost

effortless. Sudden chirp of a cell phone:
electronic shiver rippling the grass.

Without even thinking, I answer from
a sunken trench, connecting to a woman

states, time zones, whole centuries away.
Just casually, in passing, she asks about

a man she doesn't know was once my lover,
doesn't know blindsided, mesmerized me.

iv.

Who doesn't desire to be mesmerized by love?
Last night beneath small-town streetlights, I watched

girls in strappy sleeves, strappy sandals,
strappy thongs trail their ponytails as they

sashayed past. Tanning bed to marriage bed:
soon they'll root, swell, grow bulbous with life.

Their lovewords linger on the breath of beebalm;
I feel my own drawl flex, bend, purr—

once more I'm Madonna of the Magnolias,
Dewey Dell Bundren, Lena Grove hitching

one last ride. Once more he calls me *whore*.
Remnants of his madness tattoo my skin,

ripen, swell, turn yellow-pink, and linger;
once more I fear the shadow of his hand.

V.

All my life's been lived in shadow, pattern
pieced by someone else: daughter, mother,

lover. *Whore.* Back home, in the house of slow
and patient death, my mother waits for me

to chat companionably about carpet moths,
Ollie and Janet adopting a dog,

the kitchen fire that flared three houses down.
There's laundry in the dryer, dirty cups

beside the sink. Slouching down the hall
in his baseball gear, my nearly teenaged son

deftly sidesteps questions he seems to lack
the words to ask: why his mother layers

scarves around her neck, trails broken-winged
across the bleachers, sobs the whole way home.

vi.

Across the Tennessee from Pittsburg Landing,
a man squats on a strip of sand baiting

fishhooks for his daughters. Cicadas whir.
Lizards scamper across the wagon trace,

carve a path uphill from the Hornet's Nest.
Raising an umbrella against the sun,

I pretend I'm an overripe Southern belle
who's driven out to see the spectacle

with a picnic basket and a lady's maid
for propriety. I watch the shades of boys

unformed, inarticulate as my own son
colliding on this accidental field:

bullets fly through the Peach Orchard, dropping
snow-white petals on the dead, the dying.

vii.

So many battles are accidental. Love,
my son, when it finally comes—unlooked-for,

savage, bursting riotous into bloom,
stunning us while we lie dreaming—love's

the only thing worth fighting for. Its absence
is the wound in the heart, slit in the skin

of the universe through which we fall and, falling,
are lost. What we mean when we say *evil*:

hammer-cocked, breath-holding moment in
the young and unstained orchard. Iron fingers

tightening around a rifle stock,
tightening around a woman's throat.

Sudden spatter of gravel as a car
skedaddles down the petal-flecked road.

V.

Phantom Limb

First the doctors peel my flesh,
expose the bone, saw it smooth.
Working in layers, they mold muscle,
snug up tissue to cushion the stump,
snip skin in overlapping flaps
exactly the way you'd wrap a present,
pleating sudden ridges and angles.
And then, prosthesis: liner, socket,
foot. I'll walk, all right: you'll notice
nothing amiss, unless you're watching
in the evening hour, when shapes
branch off in doorways, two by two—
you'll see me stumble on the side
he always took, while in the houses
doors bang shut, lights flick on.

Mrs. Pinkerton Charts the Stars

My story's written there: the ways I found
to cling to him, to listen to his lies.
Nothing I'd learned had taught me how to live:
a genteel smattering of tongues, how
to play a polonaise, to thread a hatpin.
Against his fingers' paralyzing crawl
across my skin I sprawled defenseless, salty
trickle from my thighs complicit in
the pin and rip of canines (always that line:
pain before pleasure, pleasure won't begin).
I'm awkward, late apprenticing; still,
I haunt the flying bridge all night, resolved
at last to master some navigating skill,
to swing the sextant, situate myself.

Mrs. Pinkerton Finds Her Sea Legs

"Sotto il gran ponte del cielo
non v'è donna di voi più felice."
— *Cio-Cio-san (Butterfly),* Madama Butterfly, *Act III*

He told me on the ship, of course. He said
he'd never loved her, simply taken her
in passing, lovely blossom for his pleasure.
"Real marriage," he said, smiling, "is when like
marries like." All voyage he was speaking
of his future: he burned to be a captain.
How he'd fill the house with narwhal tusks,
gold ingots, giant mollusks. Ambergris.
How his sons would follow him to sea.

I gloried in his vision, loved to hear
the sailors call me "Mrs. Pinkerton."
I never thought of her at all, not
the days I lay sick in the cabin, not
the nights I masked my ache, my nausea,
as he taught me how to be a woman.
And when we anchored ship in Nagasaki,
first flush of spring veiling the trees, myself
unveiling—bride, wife—it seemed to me

as if no other woman walked the earth.
Even as I waited in her garden,
saw my husband pause before her door,
it seemed simple, like shedding skin. By then,
they'd told us of the child, his golden curls,
how his name meant "sorrow" in Japanese;
my husband vowed to raise him American.
I felt how fine a man my husband was,
promised I'd love his son just like my own.

Around me the trees were bare, fresh-clipped; the shell
of a blue-speckled egg crunched beneath
my heel. And then I saw my husband running,
running away from me. Was love the thing
that goaded me toward her door—terrible need
to see myself reflected in her eyes?
What came after was nothing: child wailing across
the ocean, husband mewling at my breast
night after bloodshot night. Her neatly scissored throat.

Mrs. Pinkerton Interprets Local Custom

"Potete perdonarmi, Butterfly?"
— Kate Pinkerton, Madama Butterfly, Act III

kneeling now before you
head bowed body blanched

correct in silk the heft
and texture of atonement

hair of silvery gold
lacquered back to display

my shameful foreign face
circles of my eyes

powdered to disguise
the black-purple stains—

how can i bear your pity
i who enter your house

bringing pain with me?
you say our sons are born

blind their wings too frail
to fly you say no man

will think to save them if
women pleasure themselves

by pecking out one
another's bird-bright eyes

A Receipt to Cure Mad Dogs, or Men or Beasts Bitten by Mad Dogs

Communicated by Sir Rob. Gourdon, ca. 1690

Agrimony roots, Primrose roots,
Dragon roots, Single Peony roots,
the leaves of Box, of each a Handful;
the Starr of the Earth, two handfuls;
the black of Crabs' Claws prepared,
Venice Treacle, of each one ounce:
all these to be beaten and bruised together
and boiled in a Gallon of Milk
till the half be boiled away,
then put into a Bottle, unstrained,
and given, 3 or 4 Spoonfuls at a time,
to the Dog or Beast or Man
three Mornings together
before new and full Moon.

Fig

তুমি যেনো ডুমুরের ফুল হয়ে গেলে.
You've become invisible like the dumur [fig] flower.
— Bengali proverb

i.

I've become the invisible flower,
inflorescence of fig-in-bloom
embroidering my inner walls.
Fleshy peduncles descend
from my rib cage, wasps colonize
my pelvis, seeking the ostiole's
warm-mouthed murmur: sex till death.
The male fig wasp develops, mates,
and dies inside the fruit of his birth.
How many men will die in me?

ii.

How many men will eat my fruit,
meditate for years beneath
my banyan bones? A parable
of the fig tree: when the branch
is tender and putteth forth leaves,
ye know that summer is nigh. Rejoice
in me, each under your own vine
and fig tree, fruit of paradise
ripening beneath the leaves
that multiply, hiding our sins.

iii.

"When I grew into my beauty,
I became a *kanephoros*
and wore a necklace of dried figs."
A woman learns to initiate
herself, leads processions to the altar
atop the acropolis, bears
the *kanoun* readied for sacrifice.
Old men tell her: "Dwell within
the temple of our beliefs, not
the wilderness that lies beyond."

iv.

What if wilderness lies within?
I sacrificed to Dionysus—
infected body and mind by him
who's also god of figs, I slew
the mountain lion, my son: you.
Cursing the fig that yields no fruit,
Jesus said, "Let no fruit grow
on thee henceforward forever"—
his fig was just a metaphor.
Every mother mourns with me.

V.

I've become the dumur flower,
favorite of monkeys, bats,
refuge of the wingless male.
When the fig wasp dies, the fruit
absorbs his body. His winged mate
carries pollen fig to fig:
women's work. Each one ripe
contains fifteen hundred seeds.
Whoso keepeth the fig tree
shall eat the fruit thereof.

Notes

"Nakhla": Nakhla is a calcium-rich igneous rock formed on Mars 1.3 billion years ago that was blasted from the Martian surface 10 million years ago. It eventually became part of a twenty-two-pound achondrite that exploded over Nakhla, Egypt, in 1911. One fragment reportedly incinerated a dog.

"Bar at the Folies-Bergère": It has been suggested that Manet associated oranges with prostitution in his paintings; it is known that Manet asked the real-life woman who worked in the bar to pose in his studio for the painting.

"A Receipt to Cure Mad Dogs, or Men or Beasts Bitten by Mad Dogs": Adapted from an account in the *Philosophical Transactions of the Royal Society of London,* vol. 16, 1686–1692.

"Fig": In ancient Greece, the *kanephoros* led the procession to a sacrifice bearing a basket (the *kanoun*) of offerings and sacrificial implements. The words spoken by the kanephoros are from *Lysistrata.*